EARTH-LIGHT

EARTH-LIGHT

1963-1982

Selected Poetry of
GWENDOLYN MACEWEN

General Publishing/*Toronto*

FIRST PUBLISHED IN 1982 BY
General Publishing Co. Limited
30 Lesmill Road, Don Mills
M3B 2T6 Ontario

CANADIAN CATALOGUING IN PUBLICATION DATA

MacEwen, Gwendolyn, 1941-
    Earthlight :   selected poetry of Gwendolyn
MacEwen, 1963-1982

ISBN 0-7736-1117-7

I. Title.

PS8525.E95E27   C811'.54   C82-094753-9
PR9199.3.M242E27

COVER ILLUSTRATION BY   ISBN 0-7736-1117-7
BRIAN HENDERSON   FIRST PRINTING
DESIGN BY E.J. CARSON   PRINTED IN CANADA

36,697

Contents

Preface

"They are burning Damascus," says T. E. Lawrence in one of Gwendolyn MacEwen's latest poems. Today the armies of the Near East threaten to burn it again.

Egypt, Israel, Jerusalem, Sidon, and Tyre, names that seemed exotic, merely poetic, when MacEwen first read her poems in Toronto coffee houses in the early sixties are now current — in museums, in board rooms, in the daily news. This development lends a certain irony to George Bowering's comment, in an early review of *The Rising Fire*, that MacEwen's work stands outside the mainstream of Canadian writing and, though a complex music, is less immediate.

True, most Canadian poets tend to pick their way through space like surveyors with a fear of heights. They cling to the representative and the representational, the documentary. They focus on civil space, perceiving the social body in terms of its material syntax of streets and roads, buildings and rooms, the tangle of hydro and communication lines. Even if they wander, we can find them on the map, anchored in immediate local detail.

Whereas MacEwen invokes a dancer in a landscape where "all maps have resigned." Vertical in vision, oracular and metaphorical in mode, she speaks of a body of identity that is not so much social — political and general, as individual — sexual and mystical. She appeals to a syntax of dance, the tangled bodies of lovers, who are also "holy athletes" — to a paradigm where the dance and the dancers are one. MacEwen's dancer is "the cipher of movement,/ a terrific code." The "cipher" is zero, its root in the Arabic "cifr," meaning "empty." Yet it is out of that moving emptiness, that terrific code, life's trillions come.

Such a vision is not apolitical. Though it does not discriminate English and French, Canadian and American, it allows her to speak with a collective voice few English-Canadian writers have managed, as when she says:

you cannot do this to them, these are my people;
I am not speaking of poetry, I am not speaking of art.
you cannot do this to them, these are my people.
you cannot hack away the horizon in front of their eyes.

The words might be equally appropriate in Spadina, Beirut, or the U.N.

Actually, MacEwen begins like a good Canadian with "Explorations and Discoveries," insisting we must sing to "master wind's loud/love of land in insistence on dimension." Pure light is void, till the yellow sun cuts out yellow dolls, makes dark, makes matter, makes space and time — the fields of violence and play.

She comprehends the boy's desire to sit with Caesar's son in the coliseum and watch the gold chariots, the games of the warlord sun. But to be bemused by power, to pursue empire over "outer space," is to invite progressive fragmentation and alienation. (Men go to the moon and miss the moonlight; they pick up rocks, and miss the earthlight flooding the lunar pools.) It is not power but comprehension we must feed.

MacEwen would have us swallow space/time, break down the subject/object distinction, and celebrate dimension as a continuous variety of unfolding "matter" — grass, clouds, constellations; dragonflies and flying machines; alphabets and hymn tunes and scientific theories. This is the darkening body of god, which we feed and we also feed on.

In a partial, merely objective view, that of technological man, everything, all of us, are but items in a supermarket, both consumer and consumed — the whale eaten by his own light.

In a more comprehensive view, we participate in a large communion, break out of our isolated egos, breakfast, if you will, on the one great peanut butter sandwich. (See *Magic Animals*, MacEwen's other major selection, for the full "Breakfast for Barbarians.") It is not the emperor but the man in the conical hat who, swallowing all, arrives at the comic vision.

Most Canadians, modern man, approach inner space as one would approach a Medusa's head, through the mirror of outer space, an objectivist language. We can, of course, look at madness, sex, pain, joy through the camera eye, on film. War and pornography fill our screens every night. Like the anonymous protagonist of a Robbe-Grillet novel, we become each a voyeur of fear and desire, of what might be our lives. It looks immediate, but it is highly mediated, alien.

MacEwen rejects this distancing, would internalize all possible experience, to be able to speak of it, not with analytical, objective knowledge, but with biblical knowledge. To say then what most will not, that we are ambiguous, that our exorbitant hungers and satisfactions are both erotic and holy, that their incestuous relations may spawn a bestial phantasmagoria or project an angelic visitation, the god, muse, lover crashing with darkening will and brightening knees in real sheets — "oh/dark outrageous anchoring" — this, surely, is immediate speech.

Yet it does not exclude descriptive tact, as in MacEwen's "One Arab Flute." Here is the journalist's East as few journalists could see it, a record of sense. And a kind of prophetic vision emerges simply from what is, a Bedouin boy playing to himself as he watches his sheep.

at sundown past Beersheba
and the flute he played
was anarchy between his fingers;
I saw the poor grass move
its tender blades, I
heard the wind awakening
the desert from its sleep.

But, again, it is not oil or the collisions of empire that are of ultimate interest. Beyond dimension MacEwen asks poetry to speak of the unspeakable, as in "The Absolute Room" mere documentary may speak to the "wondrous nothing" that fills a room, and everything else. And, as the Arabs imply to Lawrence, it may be failure and not success that sets us free there — to empty ourselves and become full.

So Lawrence, despite the apparent success of a long campaign, no longer cares. "They are burning Damascus," he says. And he falls asleep.

D. G. Jones
1982

Acknowledgements

'The Carnival' and 'Animal Syllables' are reprinted from *The Fire-Eaters* by permission of Oberon Press.

All poems from *The T. E. Lawrence Poems* are reprinted by permission of Mosaic Press/Valley Editions.

THE
RISING FIRE

Exploration and Discovery

We must sing much to master wind's loud
love of land
in insistence of dimension,
and be bards ever
on green earth under
clear-cut sun cutting yellow dolls of us
in the morning.

In an orphan valley between
two tossed parental mountains
boys blow reed pipes where the water is
and string days around their necks
like painted beads;
in a city's rabbit hours
in lightning streets three children
trisect a dragonfly, taste air on their tongues
and find it sweet and run after wind,
their hands wide open like beggars.

A white bonhomme smokes the years in his pipe;
his woman knits socks for the feet in her daughter's womb;
day like a blond bear leans down their shoulders.

There are sixteen sails on the sea's face.
The waves drink the water.
A moon is happening in the high sky
and the grass prays greenly.

The butter of the sun is spread on world
thick as all summer in this time.
All gay seeds are split for primordial light
to enter.
            Welcome to the earth.

Arrows

arrows, you
lie at right angles
to yourselves,
being a double compass
or a crisscrossed anatomy
or any metaphor on top of that.

arrows, you
enjoy being equivocal;
look I will humour you —
(your ankles point east
and west and all directions;
there is a panther in
your garden, and so on)

what you
do not know is
that I can play the game
excellently (light,
lines of light glance off
the angles of your form;
we will speak of stars
and crossbows if you like)

arrows, your
arm was a tangent
to suns which were love
and your leg was a tangent
to moons which were hate;
I will let you be
equivocal.

arrows, you
are careless and beautiful
and do not hurt deliberately —
(I will play the game
and will not speak
of the directions of love;
they may confuse you)

The Death Agony of the Butterfly

a monarch beat its velvet brain
against the light, against
the cold light, I
thought of you.

dance you, dance
you bitch
against the light against
the cold light, that's
what you said.

always behind me, always
behind me is
your violent music, beat
until the butterfly's velvet brain
is dead.

dance you, dance
you bitch, I
love you against
the light against
the cold light, always
behind me is
your violent music.

Two Horses

I saw two horses yesterday
pulling a cart through the world of men

and stopping in the midday street
to nip and lick each other's flanks

and something about them there was pitiful
— a kind of futility difficult to name —

it may have been they could not mate
for each unto the other was
too strongly chained.

The Double Horse

evening they
stand sideways
in leaning sleep; evening
flank to flank
in parallel sleep they
are one horse
with heads at each end;
now watch them;
the thing beyond the poem
joins them

Black and White

you wore it you wore the night
strapped like black wings to your white
arm you came as in an inverse film
of bright alarm and darkening will
of knees which crashed the sheets
of shoulders which descended
                              and
descended down and crashed from flight
in interchanging black and white

crash crash fly down bird fly down
in bright absurd alarm as the dove
the bird at the loins the love
plummets down to me and
now fly down black and white fly down
beacon and the brilliant knees
                              oh
dark outrageous anchoring and the beauty of it

Skulls and Drums

you talked about sound, not
footstep sound, shiphorn, nightcry,
                               but

strings collecting, silver
and catgut, violas riding
the waves of May like soft ships,
                               yes

and the anchoring senses,
the range, the register,
the index
        in the ear, the long
measure from the drums of our skulls
to the heart (and its particular tempo);
the music anchored there, gathered
in.

you will hear me now, I think,
while my skin still gathers tones of the sun in,
while we ride the bars, the slow passages
of these first minutes,

while the taut drums of our skulls
open
and all sounds enter
and the pores of our skin like slow valves open.

we will hear each other now, I think,
while nothing is known, while sound
and statement in the ear
leave all alternatives;
                     our skulls like drums,
                     like tonal caves
                     echo, enclose.

while the ribs of our bodies are great hulls
and the separate ships of our senses
for a minute

anchor.

for a minute in the same harbour

anchor.

The Harbour

but the city across the harbour from me
drones on daily its monotone music
        while I am remembering yesterday
and china being broken on
        the floor of your small room;
each crash was an antiphony to
        the breaking of your images;
your hands lifted the plates like babies
        and flung them for
the cruel beauty of my vision in you —
        (wanting rather safety, laughter
or the blind bone which need not ever break) —
        and you, you with your halfway
armoured vision cracking like armadillo after
        the gravity of our coupling
continued breaking with perfect precision
        breaking the dishes
        and watching yourself break them —

I know and I know and today the city
as I cycle home through the gulls and rockpiles
        sleeps past the bay
on its strange grey music
        and somewhere you
are there behind the walls of it
        and though I cannot hear
in the anchoring distance, I know
        that you are throwing dishes
in the small room over and over
        forever and ever
and watching them break —
and amazed at their breaking —
and watching yourself break them —
and thinking of gulls and rockpiles —

Inquiry into Time

The little boy has left the crowd,
left your tight handclasp
at noon in nineteen-sixty.
Where has the little boy gone?

You have given him mint and wishes.
It does not matter.
You have given him large toys and large love.
It does not matter. He does not want them.

The little boy has gone to the coliseum
to watch the gold chariots.
He has gone to gaze on red Roman nostrils
of rare Roman horses.

Why did the little boy go? from your hand?
out of the crowd?
You have given him custard and bicycles.
And it does not matter. He does not want them.

He heaved his ball into the coliseum
and has gone to sit with Caesar's son
and watch the gold chariots; I told you.

You have given him scooters and embroidered pillows.
It does not matter.
He has centuried away from you
to play ball in gold-toned Rome
and sit with Caesar's son above the chariots.

The hands on your clock melt like a Dali,
worried that one boy
has seen through their pretense.
Then you must melt also, here in the one noon,
melt like that clock, like that boy's clock
to follow him.

Eden, Eden

it is the thunder is
the vocal monument
to the death-wished rain,
or obelisk in a granite sky
that roars a jawed epitaph
through cut cloud.

in the morning
thunder is the reared stone elephant,
               the grown element of grey;
its trunk is vertical and thick as thunder;
the elephant stubs down the wrenched lightning,
funnelling a coughed verse
for the suicidal rain
in the morning.

the stormed man is heavy with rain
and mumbles beneath the elephant gargle
and his jaw locks human in the rain,
and under the unlocked jaw of the cut sky
and under the bullets of the elephant's trunk

he is thinking of a thunder garden.

behind sense he is thinking of a warped tree
with heavy fruit falling,
peaked rock fighting the ragged fern
in the other storm's centre,
a monolithic thunder tree
and a man and woman naked and green with rain
above its carved roots, genesis

The Two Themes of the Dance

One: God is a Dancer

removed from the sticky pews
of the skull's cathedral, he,
almost anonymous dances
for Zarathustra and
the sweaty Hassid
and others; pirouettes among
the mountains, O foots
and forms disarmingly diced
ages of ice for the Samson
and the snowman of our tribes,
for the scabby knees of saints
in sad perpetual genuflections —
the dancing god,
the one who dances outward

Two: Adam is the Dancer in Reverse

but he dances into himself,
not outward,
dances down his own throat
in a strange muscular utterance
which stutters of tendons
and internal rhythms, delicate
fables of the flesh and
I watch him as I would watch
sundancers with the hot mind
pulling the dawn from my marrow

watch with the hot mind tracking
that inverted dancer
who twists through a jungle of innocents
through the choreography of Gehenna
or the backward landscapes of Zarathustra
in a concave ballet where
with grace and desperation he
dives down his own gut
and squeezes
as if his organs
were the other kind

The Hand

to wear the whole cosmos like a conical hat
with the raw brain set under it, behind eyelight
of bright and wild brown, is comical
for the closed academies and other square
structures with venetian windows in the skull
called Limited Visions Incorporated
and go by other names...
                              but
we wear it; it is light; argue with gravity
and are embryonic, even as eggs ignite
fires as comets' oval orbits in the brain
and again and again your seed is fire
in the vision of your thighs,
is reason for the bright mindseye
to let the birthdays of your sight recur...
                              Ah
clarions and horses!

at first you were some satyr
in the fields of my need and
the sylvan eye turned on me for
other fires, but now wands waver
at our wrists the wave-length of flutes
and you in your uproarious calmness
grace me in the chaos of these places,
uproot me for freedom and clarity
and uproarious innocence...
                              O
hold hold the moment which is horror
in my hand for the world is within it
and the mind is finally a black satyr wrestling
for varieties of berries and sylvan fevers
in the denseness of its forests forever...
                              grace it,
that trace of our need for silence
among clarions and horses and brilliant cities
and keep in order the questions of our coming
when evening on an island we sleep
with all reason folded under the knees
or traced like bracelets on the wrist
and love is several realities also...

                                  or give me
a clearness, a quietness of fires
with the complex sky traced above our brows
for now we sleep in the midnight of least reason
and the complex jigsaw cosmos
is a conical hat simply
for we are magicians and argue with gravity,
the satanical mandrake in the core of our madness;
for we are magicians in the nights of our seasons
and your hand is the world; it is my hand; a moment
and your hand is the world; it is horror; and beauty

A BREAKFAST
FOR BARBARIANS

The House

in this house poems are broken;
I would invent the end of poetry;
we are only complete when

that image of me in you
that image of you in me
breaks, repairs itself.

you are the earth and the earth;
release those cosmic hands which held you
while I set out on my urgent journeys —

in this house we repair
torn walls together and do not
ask how they were torn.

we work slowly, for
the house is the earth
and the earth —

the delicate people in you
move
from room to room.

The Cyclist in Aphelion

approach it, neither a place nor a time but a state
    of hotness; approach it on large wheels;
    I am the red centre
    the scream of quinine in the ear
    I am the hot pain at your heels

now your worried feet pivot fall to summer
    the cycles are sped up
    and swift is your speech
    as the rasping zodiac of your spokes;
    you are a constellation of bicycles

to reach me is to burn first
    you cannot come if you fear fire;
    I want you to teach me how to sleep
    to brand me with the violent suns of your coming
    to reach me in aphelion

to violate twilight, to inherit the earth
    blind even, and backwards
    to become a craftsman with an iron mask
    who welds a terrible braille of poetry
    which burns if you read it with your fingers

approach it, a state of hotness
    approach it on large wheels;
    I am the red centre
    the scream of quinine in the ear
    I am the hot pain at your heels

The Kindled Children

in summer you invoked a fire for children;
you aimed a small lens at the sun and kindled a twig
beneath it; you had that much time to do it —
that much of a magnified afternoon for the children's kindling.

now this innocence confounds me, this ability to stand
hours beneath the prolonged sun, expanding light
in the exploding novum of their eyes, and
without anger at the world's turn, its argument into night.

impossible to know where your anger lies!
in my burning world I must protract time
down to the worlds of my fevered hands
holding knives to carve the lithic minutes of my lines.

and in the kindling unquiet of my brain I recall
all kinds of burning times — a night in fall
when suns went silently nova, light years beyond
your unlit room, and other times, but always the burning

ensues upon my watching you, in summer and in other seasons
when you do not argue the day into night, as I do —
when you hook a whole afternoon into a small lens
and change it into fire for the kindled children,
when you move about, having little need
of wider fires, whole burning worlds, or anything
beyond the intact moments of your deeds.

You Cannot Do This

you cannot do this to them, these are my people;
I am not speaking of poetry, I am not speaking of art.
you cannot do this to them, these are my people.
you cannot hack away the horizon in front of their eyes.

the tomb, articulate, will record your doing;
I will record it also, this is not art.
this is a kind of science, a kind of hobby,
a kind of personal vice like coin collecting.

it has something to do with horses
and signet rings and school trophies;
it has something to do with the pride of the loins;
it has something to do with good food and music,
and something to do with power, and dancing.
you cannot do this to them, these are my people.

Between You and Me

Between you and me the Messiah stands
like a white and wild chaperone;
our hands are joined onto his hands
and we cannot go anywhere alone.

I know your body by virtue of his flesh
and your words by virtue of his interpreting tongue
and you know me by the same process
and will know me thus for long and long.

We are very aware of his slightest move
and he records every place we three have been;
we are very aware of his going out,
of his going out and of his coming in.

Safed: Israel

Now
the almond eye of the mule
regards Safed sideways
and with some mistrust
as in a Chagall
where bodies and the discs of spines
are in free fall, and the shrines
of memory are torn by the eye
turned sideways, back. In all things
we lack the final syntax, the total form.
The eye is not full on Safed.

Between mosques and the breasts of Miron —
Tombs. Shammai. Hillel. Cabbala
is the coil at the student's ear, is
the mystic disc of the spine
which rattles for the Torah dance
under the old man's eye, is
the large flower behind the heel
everyday.

     Once
the Eye turned full on Safed
and wrestled for the light with
that total and sarcastic dark,
and won the jacob-angel fight.

     Now
old men have flowers at their heels
under the toasted sundown stone
before sudden turquoise doors:

     Now
the almond eye of the mule
regards Safed sideways.

         ISRAEL 1962

Tel Hazor Excavation

Always
we draw that line between form and void
and step across it solemnly
as though each day were genesis
and it is.

      Sabbath we climbed Tel Hazor
in a seedy wind, was hot and high;
we know only the quick inquiry,
the familiar hinge of a door
where no door is.

          On top in the High Place
where the temple was, you have the blood-let
(a fact, take it from there);
you have tips of towers which keep sinking,
you stoop in the streets of Sisera (think) —

Think in terms of time; grip this —
imagine an archaic door,
an apology for the naked hinge,
and then step back behind it, Ari.
We have only this, the quick
inquiry.

      ISRAEL 1962

Thou Jacob

'. . . . . the sacred king was ritually lamed in a way
that obliged him to swagger or lurch on high heels. . . '
ROBERT GRAVES: THE WHITE GODDESS

thus the shrunken sinew, the dislocated hip
got from angel-wrestling or standing, legs split
between a moving vessel and a static bank, or dangling,
the hair bound up in oak trees; terrible to be divine
like this and therefore possessing, for instance,

a magic heel one should not tread upon;
some parts of the king are too beautiful for use,
so loose the precious muscle in the thigh,
destroy the high white brow where cobras curl;
be delicate, my king, and very lame, O Thou
Achilles, Thou Jacob of my dreadful dream.

For Hart Crane

the images, the images removed ten times
and taut as cables straddling
gaps of strange tension, find finally
reality crutched in the Bridge's armpits
or in the charged spaces between breaths —

the sun, tho, pinpoint and tidy on sundays
is no consolation; the combless hair of waves
erases vision; ferneries fumble
clarity; you alone have watched steel crumble.

now I speak of you as your own kingdom,
ruling an empire of conglomerate provinces
from an undersea,

as, sick of focus
on a blind skyline, a crashed circumference,
your neck was free to bend from that swaying deck
down, down to the crazy heaven of the fishes.

The Peanut Butter Sandwich

We are dangerous at breakfast, at breakfast we
      investigate the reasons for our myths
viciously, and at breakfast we need no reasons
      for being; we are

Solemnly eating our thick sandwiches
      and knowing the highest mysticism
is this courageous breakfast and us at it
      concentrating
      conscious

Of our outrageous reality. The sandwich!
      The peanut butter sandwich!
A symbol of itself only, and you beautiful
      across the table, eating.

But caught in this cliché of a breakfast
      and knowing it too, we speak
loudly: 'Feed me some symbolisms!
      I want a dragon sandwich!'

'I am freight train, sea-wind and raspberry jam!'
'I am snow, tiger and peanut butter!'

Alas, we have too many myths
      and we know that too. But it is breakfast.
I am with you. Care for another?

The Winemaker
for Al Purdy

the winemaker comes to Toronto
the urgent winemaker comes
        from a little rural cottage
comes to Toronto (can't stand the place just
        passing through)
with fingers dyed a deep magenta from the stubborn grapes
with one foot on the pavement
and the other poised for flight —

the winemaker invades Toronto
and the city ignites under his heels
        and in a few hours he has accomplished
everything and condenses all possible
        appointments into urgent minutes wherein
the entire history of Canadian poetry
is brought up to date over tavern draught
        or that purple homemade stuff
that dyes the guts a deep magenta —

the winemaker comes to Toronto
        disguised as a dervish to chase himself
back and forth across the urgent purple city, a living query
of his own movement — like those poems of his that go
        round and round and where they stop nobody
guesses —

the winemaker comes to Toronto
(can't stand the place just passing through)
        and leaves a pile of urgent
poems in his wake and leaves again
        for the little rural cottage
back to the deep magenta twilight of Ameliasburg
to write those poems that turn and keep turning

        (there is the man; he returns,
        he is always   returning)

The Sperm King

'That mortal man should feed upon the creature
that feeds his lamps . . . and eat him by its own light . . .'
　　　MELVILLE: MOBY DICK

the king pours oil for our anointing
as fire coils, and loins flash tides;
we thrash, our flesh is fish
in the foamed oceans of our night —
(let the seed of the king erase the sea,
his burning perfume be our light)

the sharks　　the carcass
the food　　the flesh
the fire　　the seed
the sea　　the light

O ocean, boil in his throat!
from his terrible mouth his millions spill;
sperm burns in the wake of the fragrant whale;
massive as of seas is the throw and the thrash of it

(dark mouths of thy sharks
with backward smiles
shake, hard on thy death, insatiate)

erase thou this
dark shark of my mouth;
the eye dives, blind with light,
into an incoherent sea —
(dive then, dive to the depths of me,
as that proud one runs his loud tons down,
fragrant and terrible,
to smash his outraged crown)

Eyes and Whales

leave the blood to its own reasons for being;
(how often have I looked inward
to find my own bleary eye
looking back out)?
for in those weary seas which trespass sense
the diving eye sometimes collides with
great blue whales of innocence.

> (a whale once, blue or sperm,
> I am not sure which,
> entangled itself in
> a transatlantic cable
> cutting off communi
> cations between 2 continents)

leave the blood to its own reasons for being;
(forget those breathing seas, horrible electric
seas, little squeezed amoeba beasts,
voltages of jellyfish, jealousy of fish,
graphs of waves, blood tides, lunar
madness; let me walk on beaches
clean as the complex sea,
the sea which is the sea's own tale)

forget this backwash of vision,
this tangled cable from sense to sense,
the diving eye colliding with many blue
whales.

Finally Left in the Landscape

Finally left in the landscape is the dancer;
    all maps have resigned, the landscape has
designed him. My lines can only
    plagiarize his dance.

    Moving, he is the cipher of movement,
    a terrific code;
    witness him.

Now I seek him, nor rely on chance;
I turn stones and find broken glass
like pseudo-suns in the broken sand,
intense for their size —
(are they from his fallen eyes)?

Life, your trillions people me;
I am a continent, a violated geography.
Yet still I journey to this naked country
to seek a form which dances in the sand.
This is my chosen landscape.
Hear my dark speech, deity.

The Aristocracies

You are born with these in your blood—
natural aristocracies, not power aristocracies
as the world sees them, but natural aristocracies
evident from the curve of the mouth, from the stance.

The title you confer upon yourself, a pre-occupation
with eagles, a passion for gold, for mountains,
for that which is super-natural, superlative,
grants you your maps and your kingdoms.

Let it be understood that this is not art,
this is not poetry; the poetry is
the breathing air embracing you,
the poetry is not here, it is elsewhere
in temples, in territories of pure blue.

Behind my eye a diagonal arabic music
insists I censure dimensions; I think
in cross-sections of sound, flat arabesques;
love, I think you have become a bas-relief.

Can you not break from this censured landscape?
I waste each blue breath from my mouth
and I cannot recover the exiled minutes of my life—
(ruthless and royal blue, the profiles of kings
confound me)

The body of God and the body of you
dance through the same diagonal instant
of my vision. Let this be the end of argument,
O crowned and captive dancer, let me not argue
your flesh to death.

You must dance forever beneath this heavy crown
in an aristocratic landscape, a bas-relief of living bone.
And I will altogether cease to speak
as you do a brilliant arabesque within the bas-relief,
your body bent like the first letter
of an unknown, flawless alphabet.

THE
SHADOW-MAKER

White is Every Colour

Tonight your eye is utter snow
and we have moved through worlds
of ice to reach
this frozen gaze and go
beyond the spectrum of our days

For this we drained dreams
of their red miracles and seeds
and rode the moving icebergs
of our deeds and splendid bones

(*Listen*, the marrow whispers
now the white blood answers
now the white mind sees)

We stole the colours of the world —
the blue of royal, unreal seas,
the blood that writes the name
of night between the sun and sun

The green of days between
the night and night, and took
this stolen spectrum far away
to crush it into utter white

We have misplaced our darkness, and
on such a night as this we know
we are the victims
of something beautiful
and multi-coloured as the snow

Invocations

In this zoo there are beasts which
like some truths, are far too true —
(clawing ones, and fire-breathers
and flesh-rakers like piranhas
and those that crush the bones to chalk
and those that bare their red teeth in the night)
and some shoot fire to melt the snow
and some chew lazily
on continental shelves,
and some wrap themselves around the world
in an embrace which does not kill
but invents new life around the wound.

Therefore I invoke you, red beast
who moves my blood,
demon of my darker self,
denizen who crawls in my deep want,
white crow, black dove,
eagle and vulture of my love;
and you great buzzard of my dreams,
I call you down
out of yellow rocks and pools of salt,
desert temples hollowed out,
and you white ghost who dwells
in the corner of my eye
to see those things I cannot see
(the broken edges of the air,
the flicker of forms before they occur)

But I invoke you all too well
and you are all too true;
a dragon scares me into heaven,
a fish spits out the continent of Mu,
a big snake recoils and goes to sleep.

I pray the Lord my soul to keep.

The Pillars

'Since you are properly a clod,
*   you will not rise into the air;*
You will rise into the air
*   if you break and become dust;*
If you break not,
*   He who molded you will break you.'*
                    from the DIVAN of RUMI,
                    Persian poet and dervish

When all the world's supports gave way
I constructed pillars very tall indeed
(as time, or taller)
Making me the roof of all things
To keep the sky out and the awful rains —
(not to be left with nothing beneath,
even a needle's head where
with uncountable angels
one can dance)

But I feared the green earth
And its largeness, the sea-tides
I never saw except in sleep,
Distances, and purple castles in the night,
Sunflowers, conquests, kingdoms, stars;
And once fearful I no more wanted
Sunflowers, conquests, kingdoms, stars,
But that priceless loss of things —
The unbearable dark and sweet lack of wanting,
The death in the mouth, the utterly empty eye,
The easy wealth of nothing for it needs
No tending and no holding.

I said, the House of my Blood has fallen;
I said, someone with a gleaming axe
is hacking to shreds my old horizons

But now when all the world's supports give way
As they tend to do several times a day,
I construct provisional pillars very tall indeed
And invite the breaking, anytime, of these.

The Taming of the Dragon

Once the monster's jaws unfolded fire
But now how harmless are his claws
And all his teeth are capped with gold;
I can't believe they were the cause

Of all that blood. As the last ghastly strand
Of flame unravels from his mouth, I brood
The loss of the beast and how I used to stand
Stricken white in his dreadful breath.

But now the beast is taming, and beneath
His noble claw I lie, crying to death
The end of his killing, and between his teeth
Are bits of flowers, for he's sworn off flesh;
He seems so glad and foolish, and around his neck
There is a wreath.

The Naming Day

The time has come
and I have not yet named myself;
there are so many names to choose from,
there are so many names to choose from,
     and some people I know chose
     dozens, and dislike them now
and cannot cast them off, and wish
they had slept on Naming Day.

If I check a mirror
my ego will merely
eat the glass; if I ask
the wind (Speak my name
     you swift Narcissus)
it will only laugh. I know
that once I speak, the word
will sound forever through the earth.

I heard all the names
the world suggested, loud ones
and soft; I considered them
carefully before I cast them off,
     retaining only those
     which echoed back to birth.
Now desperate, I consult the melting
children in the playgrounds of
the world (May I take
     one giant step? Yes
     you may)
and get all tangled
in their plastic ropes. (Look
this is my Naming Day. What
can we tell you, what
can we say)?

(The one that you choose must be
secret and unspeakable, divine,
the gold house of your soul, and
the first word that made the world;
    whoever owns it
    will also own you.
Take care, then,
whom you tell it to)

I walked in the world and called
all things by my first inaccurate
name, yet I have heard its sound
so often that it has become
unknowable and unforeseen.
    I know that when
    this day is over
I will have chosen it again.

The Celtic Cross

As the secret lens held in your eye
Grants you a certain sight
    by covering the eye,
So I must keep and hold
The forms of loss, all I possess,
    close to my flesh to cover me,
And I'm obsessed by symbols like
    a circle or a Celtic cross.

Once you dropped the lens, and cupped
In your hand it was a world of water
    or a floating fallen sun
Like the Eye of Ra that first made man;
So I shed myself, drop
    suns from my eye
And cover the eyelids of the world with signs
    —crosses, circles, stars —
To seal somehow the forms just as they are.

But a film I saw once confessed me best
    — flowing water which erased
    (very silently, in Ireland)
A Celtic cross.

The First Poem After Rain

After the storm the strange light is
the reason for the storm; no one remembers
thunder, but embers of numb light
remain in the programs of memory.
(Outside me ruthless songs play on, play
chaos which is singular and unrepeatable;
O my teacher teach these unspeakable wrongs,
devices of life and time and storms)

After the storm the strange light is
the reason for the storm, and so it is
that life does not fail me yet I fail life
in the looking and seeking of things
which cannot come again; I sing my years out
of a thin, enduring flute, and play it while
the rain resounds, and play it for the coming
of that after-light; nor is it now an answer
which I seek, but the merest character of dream,
the least name of the nearest secret in my time,
before, during, but mostly after rain.

The Thin Garden

Lean and geometric kings take shape
on all the pillars of my sleep;
dark hands and sideways eyes
are a fiction or an accurate lie,
for I am a citizen first of all, of snow,
though the Nile floods
the deltas of my sense.
No traveller comes here from innocence
but for that myth the snow cannot provide,
and all our histories lie outside.

Here the morning is a world of palms and cocks
and between the trees a naked unreal sun goes;
birds among mangoes sing
and handsome dogs bark down all day
the boat of the sun to night.
Egypt is this thin garden I come to after
winter and a thousand years of sleep.

(camels, cafes, the awful sun,
the morning horns of Cairo and the peasants' drums)

A dragoman sold me some stone and said
'Lady, what pleases you also pleases me,
but *five piastres* only? Give me another five
for luck! This piece is from the *very top* —
This is alabaster from
the summit of *el Harm* !'

Egypt is this thin garden I come to after
winter and a thousand years of sleep,
and if it pleases you it pleases me
to wear part of the pyramid as a charm.
                              Cairo, 1966

The Fortress of Saladin

son et lumière are spirits here
that draw the ramparts of my inner city down;
why else would I tremble as the lights play on?
the pastel castle and its changing stone
reduce the fortresses of my blood to mere
tricks of light and sound

these walls have grown too tall, and I
can not hold out longer behind the towers
of the dread palace I rule from; my eye
sends shifting light to melt the walls
and one word from my mouth will end this place

below *Muqattam* the city dares not sleep
                                Cairo, 1966

One Arab Flute
Israel 1962

1.

I was innocent as a postcard
among the dark robes and bazaars;
my exiled smile shone under
the stern judicial sun;
     I drank Turkish coffee
     in the divided city
with a singular lack of irony
over the sunken tomb of Herod's family
with lovenotes scribbled on the wall
     (O really, this was also
     a British bomb shelter? Well
     well...)
and saw the tomb of Akiva
who was stripped by the iron
combs of Rome, Maimonides'
cold white cone with candles
at the bottom and the top,
     a place called Lifta
where the mouths of houses ate
the sunset, a blue-eyed Arab
with a wild profile, standing
in front of blond stone, the
blue-eyed sky over Jerusalem,
     an old artist Ephraim
     with platefuls of grapes
     and a large gaudy studio
in Safed, who was very angry
and painted noisily daily and nightly
on the mystic hills,
     a Maccabean tomb for a man
     called Yason, carved
     with caramel deers,
and my camera eye,
the curious film, the tourist
lens, followed
the old stones skyward.

2.

The kites, the coloured kites of Jaffa
were insolent in the sky;
      an old dead sweet smell
      and the peacock sea
      upheld them
and the parachute sun became
a pavilion and a distant throne;
I walked through pink tiles,
difficult shells, sandstone,
      and everyone asked the time
      on the beach at Jaffa
but the walls had gone down,
the walls of Jaffa,
and I saw the sea
through many naked doors;
      the kites like signals
      pointed sideways skyward
and Arab children screamed to find
bleached fish skulls like
a thousand heads of Jonah
on the shore.

3.

Now through a park of palms and cocks
I come to Capernaum, reading a pamphlet
that lists Christ's miracles
like adventure serials; I pray
to the pillars standing sad
as dolmens: Hold
      the sky up forever, Amen.

Now through a park of palms and cocks
I come to Kefer-Nahum; the priest
draws a crucifix through the sweat
on my brow, and hands me
      a small grey skirt
to remind my naked western knees
that this place is holy, and I
dissolve into the scenery.

4.

Kids skip rope behind the Roman arch
in Ein Karem where the light
is graded on the terraced hills;
      there are many cats and flowers,
      bells,
and a small girl carries a loaf
of bread that reaches to her knees
and all the children come and gaze
into my camera
though some are afraid to come
too near; behind them there's a sign
which reads: *John the Baptist*
was born here. I seem to see
in a small boy's face
a look that says:
      he who will come after me
      will bless this time, this
place.

5.

The workers at Ramat Rachel
have eyes at their fingernails
and they scratch dynasties from stone;
      no one can tell them
that what they find in the itchy dirt
is more than the day's few *lira*,
      (ruins of Judah's kings,
      mosaic floors)
for they are history, while we,
the disinherited, search here,
      scramble like the lizards
in the Byzantine church nearby,
scratch little marks all over
the holy floors, seeking
our reward.

6.

To reach Jerusalem you ride
through ribs of dead jeeps
and rusted wreaths of war
that line the road;
      you realize the City
      lives
because it was destroyed.
You sit by night close to
the barbed wire border; only
cats and spiders can pass; even
      the moon is divided here.
From Notre Dame the smashed
faces of Mary and Jesus
watch you with ugly irony;
      David's tower
is a conical hat in the moonlight;
the Mosque of Omar
has been there forever.
If I forget you, O Jerusalem,
may my right hand
build another.

7.

Noman's land is Gehenna
and leading from it the chalkwhite
salt of bleached houses, white-
faced, wide-eyed towns;
      children play
near Gehenna and they
are only playing, but I keep hearing
tofet drums beaten to dull
their screaming
      as when, on the yellow grass
      under
      the awful shadow of Gehenna
they lay outstretched before
the hands of Moloch
and his mouth of fire,
and waited for the sacred knife
to spill their sweet blood over.

8.
In Rehov Yafo
in the New Jerusalem
an Iraqi beggar I call John
        avoids curious eyes,
        watches the ground.
I see him wave away
the coins of pitying women
without even looking; the
dirty *piastres* stuffed in his fist
are enough for the day. How
solemnly he protests his station,
how
        violently he turns on them
        sometimes, cursing, his eyes
on fire; the old
American-styled suit he wears
hangs from him like a prayer.

9.
'What we must do,'
the man told me,
'Is keep them together.
That way
they are not dangerous.'
          But I have seen
          trees that grow sideways
in Esdraelon, fighting gravity;
their bark is strong
and corded with patience
and their leaves rush upwards
in incongruous dance.
          And I have seen
          bright coins worn
on foreheads, as though they told
the value of the skull —
          (fill in quickly
          the arab arch, jam it
          with stones, or make
          the roundness square;
          step
          lightly through
          the eastern music)
And this —
one young Bedouin boy leading sheep
at sundown past Beersheba,
and the flute he played
was anarchy between his fingers;
I saw the poor grass move
its tender blades, I
heard the wind awakening
the desert from its sleep.

Dream One: The Man-Fish

His hands were webbed and his hair was green;
I would give up everything and follow him
Down to the dark, improbable sea. He said,
'You will learn to swim, you will come with me!'

At the sea-gates some ferrymen ferried me through
A tunnel, asking, 'What will you do
Down there with him?' 'I do not know,'
I said, 'But it is certain I must go.'

Above his kingdom they said, 'Your hair —
It must be made so all the strands appear
To float like his. And he is called the Rey,'
They added, as my hair fanned out and floated away.

'What will you do for air? The Rey breathes
Through slits in his jaws.' 'I will leave,'
I said, "And I may drown — I do not know.'
'Have sense, you have no gills!' they said, 'Don't go!'

I left a note to my lover on land to say
I would return, but first I follow my lord the Rey.
The ferrymen frowned as deep I dived,
'But they are one and the same!' they cried.

Dream Two: The Beasts

Standing in a forest I slowly made out
(one by one, they were lost in the leaves)
Rabbits and foxes and beavers and bears
Who were sitting quietly waiting for me.

And down a path came two great beasts—
A big red tiger and a dog black as earth,
Hating each other and snarling and clawing,
Each of them wanting to get to me first.

The red one leapt forward and gazed at me long,
Then leaned on my right side, heavy and warm;
The dog followed after and leaned on my left
And I felt as mighty as a coat-of-arms.

Then a policeman came running and cried
'This is illegal!' 'What's illegal?' I said.
'It's illegal to draw two opposites together
And bring mortal enemies side by side!'

'But they forgot their hate in their love for me;
This is the meaning of peace!' I said,
But then all the animals ran away
And I turned and followed them into the wood.

The policeman pursued me, then changed his mood
And smiling he came and stretched out his hand;
I moved to shake it, but felt something click
As the handcuffs snapped shut on my wrist, my mind.

'*Nobody* brings the beasts together;
It's all illegal,' he said.

Dream Three: The Child

He was turning and turning and turning and turning
outside my window on a big unicycle
suspended in air beside a black tree.

Hey, why are you turning and turning and turning
getting nowhere fast on that wheel
when you could be talking to me?

I've always been here, turning and turning
and I'll always be here, turning and turning,
from the beginning and to the end turning,
from alpha to omega turning and turning,
and I looked and I saw it was me.

Sky-Riders

'Verily dawn is the head of the sacrificial horse,
the sun his eye, the wind his breath, universal
fire his open mouth... the stars his bones, the
clouds his flesh...'
          BRIHADARANYAKA UPANISHAD

Woman
I would rather journey down your lean breath
or down the skyways of your flesh
than ride by night these weary skies,
for in your eyes I see the death of death,
the morning of the world.
But there are many kinds of riders,
some riding wild and some riding blind
and one who cried, 'It is Accomplished!'
just before he lost his mind.

If you join me you'll become
another ghostly rider in the sky,
but perhaps we can dismount
somewhere where our myths cannot hunt
us down like falcons
with the greyhounds fast behind.

There is a nebula shaped like a horse
whose eye is the living anger of the night,
whose hoof is living light;
suns are plumes on his head, and tens
of millions of millions of miles sigh
between his hearing ears, and down
the dark light-years of his breath
black gas is squeezing inward to his death.

Imagine that the dark is the head of a horse
and the distance of the dark is years of light
where the beast grows inward from a sea of suns
and breathes and dies, yet the plumes
stay his stifled head and he is crowned.
This beast is beautiful, who chokes and rears
and makes no sound.

Man
But I rode before, I rode and fell
in love, from darkness into light,
and once a wise man said to me:
Child, your spurs are foolish stars
by night.

Onto the snows below us
I first gave up my soul
and threw myself white onto an altar
of ice, as sacrifice for
I don't know what,
and trailed white rabbits on the banks
of winter rivers, and was carried
on the white shoulders of the snow,
and sometimes I didn't know
if I was made from snow or flesh,
and my secret, darkest wish
was a world of blue ice, wilderness.

And the wise man said:
Draw back, dreamer, from your dream return;
time takes the river and the passionate altar;
time is a place where only water burns.
Lock up your tongue in a chain of gold;
a man should not tell where he has been
unless by chance another tale is told.

But we are the first riders
and we are the last; because
there is nowhere to go, I come,
and no tomorrow, I follow, and no past.

Child
A rider on a red horse, I
am the sun-child whom the world failed,
and I cry for the earth, the *earth*
which has failed and dropped away;
(my hands my eyes my heart
have also dropped away)
and the red horse who sired me
is trapped between my thighs,
coloured like soil, like my secret flesh

he runs, with stars colliding, and my spurs
cannot touch him and my reins
cannot hold him back.
Are we on the right track?

Old Man
How can we be, when the lovers lead us?
At any moment they might change their minds;
they turn the world, you see, and we
can only go completely mad or blind.
Theirs is a crazy energy like that of God
and their horses, have you noticed,
go unshod. Me, I'm a blinded rider
going ever blinder in the eye
as the unseen landscape passes by.
Whole mountains and whole seas escape me
though a hawk's wing against my cheek
is a catastrophe.
And my certain inner eye spins out
continents which are not there, skyways
which are not there, comets, frozen stars.
I seem to travel better without sight,
and they are soft and blunt, my spurs.
But now I drop the reins and fall
and give all of it up to night —
my body and the black horse, my soul,
whatever that is — but falling I am
pure light like Lucifer
and men will read wonders in my descent
and build shrines over my battered bones
and say:
Once upon a time a Horseman
dropped straight from the sky,
and it was raining death and dreams that day;
he was the Fourth Rider;
Let Us Pray.

Child
How many riders have gone down?
I fly now where I've never flown!
(the turning blood, the bleeding
clouds, am I
the world's next offering)?
We are three now, we were four;
below on earth the old man waits;

I can't ride more.
We were four, now we are three;
aging rider,
wait for me. Take me home,
you beast between my thighs;
tell them I'm coming.
Shut my eyes.

Man
I won't continue; it's far too far
and I'll go down with them, loud and soft
as a falling star. Love,
will you come after me?

Woman
What we ride rides us finally;
we were life's avengers, angels
of the end, because our spurs
were yearning wheels of time,
because we dared to ride the sky.
Could we do other
than destroy?
In your eyes I thought I saw
the death of death,
and you with me between stars hurled
were wind, were perfect breath.
Look, we were tricked and ridden
but once, O once, we were
the riders of the world.

Seeds and Stars

when touch is merest wish we swim
like fish, our seed the liquid night,
the length of seas, our first deep element
and love is the end of sleep and sight

when wish is merest touch I bend
like her whose curve is heaven over earth
and love beneath me far and far
makes of my flesh a miracle of stars

The Hollow

I never wrote from pain before
but then I saw the night-ship, star-ship
of our longing years leave this world
and all its fuel was tears

I never wrote from here before
but then I laid my head
in the hollow of your flesh
and heard unborn cities speaking,
generations speaking, signalling
from home, calling down the hollow
worlds and horns of bone

perhaps the night-ship, star-ship
will bring us back and never
ride out more;
I never wrote from here before

How Weeps the Hangman

Now the leaf the wild tree announces
is the season's sacrifice, and I
throw you all — pain, love, glory, blood
to the wind, crying *die, die, die*
for the whimpering hangman of our days,
die for the terrible love we bear.
O bless our lovers and our seasonal slaves;
the sacrifice the hooded lord demands is here.
Look, we have seen too much, you and I
and the mad embarrassed tree —
(don't ask me how much, don't *ask*)
and now our very bones are ropes of glass.
Come to me for I love thee,
saith the scaffold, saith the cross;
O hangman thy hood attracts me much —
(do not ask why, do not *ask*)
for we are only victims of
the cold lords of winter and of love,
and we don't know what amount of pain
our whimpers cause to the whining tree
or how weeps the hangman as
he does his duty to you and me.

To Say We Have Conquered

To say we have conquered
whatever enemies rose against us,
whatever god invented us as instruments of his war,
whatever secret tyrannies called our blood to cold;

To say we were turned and torn
upon the awful phases of the moon
and broken on its silver bleeding horns

Is foolish, for these are words
and the legends of the blood cannot be told.

The Return

I gave you many names and masks
And longed for you in a hundred forms
And I was warned the masks would fall
And the forms would lose their fame
And I would be left with an empty name

(For that was the way the world went,
For that was the way it had to be,
To grow, and in growing lose you utterly)

But grown, I inherit you, and you
Renew your first and final form in me,
And though some masks have fallen
And many names have vanished back into my pen
Your face bears the birth-marks I recognize in time,
You stand before me now, unchanged

(For this is the way it has to be;
To perceive you is an act of faith
Though it is you who have inherited me)

The Wings

*'Come hither, Adapa, why hast thou broken
the wings of the south wind?'*
FROM A BABYLONIAN LEGEND

*

Nameless,
This *is* the world I remember,
Called forth from floods
And torn out of rock,
Its roads paved with lava,
A copy of that other
World
I left you in with (a mountain, a beach, a horse,
     a city)

But
Why did you break all the wings of the south wind,
Why did you break all the wings of the world
To bring me home?

*

Why have I taken
    the roads that lead inward,
Why have I taken
    the roads that lead downward,
Where were all the highways of the world
When I fell among orange groves and thieves?

I was not told
Of the crimes the seasons commit;
Who warned me against
Baptism in my own blood?
Nameless, where were you when
    the earth's axis slipped
And the sun did not rise
For three full days?

And why
Did you break all the wings of the world
To bring me home?

*

It is all together now
(the beach, the city, the mountain, the horse)
Changed and restored and
Unchanged.

Come hither and
Dismantle me, Adapa,
   that I may not move.

Nameless, your name
Brings forth the floods.

THE ARMIES
OF THE MOON

I Have Mislaid Something

I have mislaid something very important
worse still
I can't remember what it is

I don't think it's
a thing or a wish or a taste or a poem

but it might be a dark street in London
where a cousin I never met
who spoke with the tongues of angels
died

he fell away from our blood like a word
and few understood the things he said

I have mislaid something very important
and possibly very large
like a castle in the Highlands
where the ghosts of my ancestors
wait with bagpipes and with horns

I have mislaid many places
in this house without history

there are so many places for places to hide

The Holy Burlesque

the very gay performer
in the Greek nightclub
has the last laugh, tho' we're in *fits*
when he does a little belly dance across the stage
crying *whoopah!* and *ellah!*
in the best tradition.
the thing is, he twirls and grinds
rather well, better in fact
than the large mammalian thing
who keeps falling over backwards
into her seventh orange veil.
which is one of the reasons why
the last laugh is Laki's.
he keeps laying bare
the grotesque gestures of a rival trade,
the girls with pointed shoes and orange brains
who parade their little lives upon the stage
with far less polish than he attains.
nobody gets right into Laki's eyes
where some primeval knowledge lingers, old
hermaphroditic dreams and Oh so lovely sins
of Sodom and Athens and East Toronto
none of us can reasonably deny.
which is to say
one laughs at Laki
as he struts and swivels and sometimes
kisses the handsome men who grace the tables
near the stage.
if we didn't laugh for heaven's sake,
if there was one minute of silence
in the Greek nightclub down the street
Laki's laugh would sound so shrill and pure
we'd fall over backwards
into our *retzinas* or our seventh orange beer
and rise, and repossess the stage
we occupied before two thousand years;
our lies in a blaze of orange veils would vanish
and the very gods might reappear.

A Lecture to the Flat Earth Society
with apologies to Alden

As president of this worthy organization
And having been entrusted with the task
Of saving the poor souls who dwell too near
The Edge of the Earth from falling into
The Primal Dark beyond,
I would like to say:

My God I've lived all my life right here
On the Rim, the Brink, the Final Boundary of fear
With the long flat continents of dreams behind me
And nothing ahead but the sweet and terrible Night
I long to fall into, but do not dare.

What can I tell you, who inhabit with me
The Very Edge of the Abyss? We have no bathysphere
To explore the depths, no means whereby we can collect
The Abysmal Eggs of those creatures of the chasm
Who dwell in darkness below our heels.

As president of this worthy organization
I want to point out, without arousing any fear
That we are doomed on this Disc which spins its insane dreams
Through space. And those of us who always lived too near
The Edge to begin with

Have the consolation of each other's company,
The certain knowledge that the Night is also beautiful,
The abundant Night which spews out constantly before us
As the rays of a half-forgotten sun strike us from behind
On our delicate and unwinged heels.

When I Think About It

when I think about it I know
with clear and terrible logic
that I have taken my life in my hands
everyday for almost thirty years,
what with drunken drivers, slippery
streets, lightning bolts, subway
trains, elevators, airplanes,
manholes, fences that can electro-
cute you in a minute, falling
wires, high winds, floods, fires,
and when I think about it
my death and yours is everywhere
and I wonder if I'm alive
by some sheer *fluke*,
or if the amazing thing is
not that accidents happen
but that sometimes they *don't*
in view of the million possibilities,
and when I think about it
everything becomes impossible,
getting across the street
is a major challenge, I take nothing
for granted, knowing I have earned
this minute by a series
of incredible stunts and manoeuvres
which, when I think about them,
require ever more time and energy
till there's little left
for anything else,
and when I think about it
I am an animal fighting
against desperate odds for sheer
survival (it starts to show
in my eyes), and when others are bored
because nothing is *happening*, I'm
on my knees thanking God that nothing
is happening, that the mad cab driver
didn't smear us all over the street,
that the plane for some incredible reason
stayed up and kept on flying,
and when I think about it
I don't know how I came this far,
or how much farther this wild luck will prevail,
or how I made it up to now, alive,
to tell the tale.

Two Aspects of the Moon

Nor could I sometimes dare to write:
the moon was a cup from which we drank
the silver milk of night.

For in this hour before the dawn
ghosts of many martyrs moan;
dark rain of war keeps falling
and our mouths are drowned.
I see your bright arm burning
like a torch in some abandoned countryside.
I witness the apocalypse of love
and understand how many died,
went up in flames
with an unrecordable cry.
Now I know why my mouth tears down your body
in a mad attempt to staunch the blood they shed.
I keep seeing bullets beneath your skin
which I try to suck away. Instead
I myself make new wounds, worse ones —
there where I thought a Roman lance tore you
just below the heart, I have left
my mouth's cruel mark.

Let this be for those who died
to give us this ambiguous hour.
Let us earn ourselves and bring them back
to earth,
if love means a murder and a birth.
Let this be a sign, for we may oneday
lie somewhere alone and slain.
This is nothing if it is not a prayer
and now in the hour before the dawn I swear
we will recall those other arms
which embraced fire and which in turn will turn
our flesh to char.
For if we can't love them in loving each other
we are unworthy of this hour and of all dawns
forever, and have no right to bear
the proud red scars of love we made.

Now could I sometimes dare to write:
the moon was a deadly scimitar beside your hair
and I woke with blood on my shoulder
from its sharp blade.

A Dance at the Mental Hospital

the imponderable agony
of *being* here, not just
in the dusty auditorium
smelling of drugs and lemonade
but in the world, alive,
and conscious, and alone
is what makes the dance so
strange;
(they are aware
someone has put them here,
no one was really invited)
the steps will knit together
some wide wound
that life has made; some wear
the furious defiant face
of a baby first forced to breathe;
others, from behind the slow glazed
smiles try valiantly to please;
still others stare
and cast wild eyes upon this gathering.

I think of the tale about the madman who believed all
the horrors of the world were committed to a single rose in the
hospital garden, and who struggled night after night to
get out and destroy the rose, and finally did, with his
hands bloody from the bars; he was good and mad as Christ,
and held the evil rose against his chest until he and it
both died at dawn.

the imponderable agony
of *being* here, of having
to have a shape, a foot, an ugly face,
a mind, a fit upon the floor
when the soul breaks out of the screeching teeth
and every nerve and muscle is screaming for release.
but now they are dancing, ah, slow as a nightmare
dances in the night across stale beds
beneath impossible stars (will there
be secret trysts tonight upon the sour stairs)?

I too must clutch the world's most beautiful and evil rose
against my chest and stare,
and cast wild eyes upon this gathering.

Letters of Water

Everything I thought to tell you has become
as worthless as an old forgotten tongue.
I open my mouth and my mouth is a gulf
where dying eagles screech and fall.
Our best and noblest desires resolved
themselves in broken songs of blood and fire.

The lost sounds of our love
have silenced and reformed my tongue, and now
a silver alphabet is floating past my eyes unreadably,
for all the secret things that we used to breathe
are some strange language no more known to me.

The letters turned to water
like the sea.

Everything I thought to tell you has become
a fluid silence flowing into time.
The lost sounds of our love,
the codes of stars,
are languages no more known to me.

The letters turned to water
like the sea.

A Letter to Charos

Lord of the midnight river, tell me

will my silver hands like fish
slip away from my lover's flesh
and will it surely come to this —
the final tunnel and the liquid kiss

did I throw my life away like so
much money thrown at the feet of singers,
did I throw my life at the feet of singers
like a coin tossed into a midnight fountain

was it all a magic act of sun and water,
was there something else I should have done instead

into whose future am I moving

my thighs, all silver with his seed
are sleek for swimming;
I see the aqueducts of death ahead

The Golden Hunger

First the savage flower of the mind opens, catches flies and tigers and locks them in. My vowels burst like the lungs of divers gone beyond their depths. How to address you, who have a hundred times renamed me? The moon is yellow and terrifically full...(They were there, just a week ago, walking)...and the pale skyscrapers are altars I have erected for the night. After the dark fell you came again to rename me, composite god; behind your fluid masks there is always something that remains the same. Not a feature, but a *cast* to which the face always returns. I watch your expressions change, I wait until they resolve themselves into the face I remember. Through the eyes of all I know one mind looks out like a dark captured animal, seeing only what it wants to see. There is the pain of the miracle amid reality.

Another mouth is drawn above your mouth, my Teacher, and two other eyes above your own. Who would believe this ghost is the permanent guest of my blood? I dreamed I found a priceless Stradivarius in my mailbox. What impossible concertos am I expected to play? The clouds have dissolved and the visited moon above me is an eye which watches as I bow.

House of Mercury

These days all those who come to me
should wear the blue of metal or the quick
silver of the sea which glints its mineral
histories — steel of blades from unknown wars,
scales like flint on the unknown fish, great
desolate wrecks of ships which set sail
for the depths, the thin grey clang of bells
calling someone somewhere, tin rivers of Aquarius.

Things that speak of forests I have long since lost
disturb me — (eyes the colour of dry moss).
Leave me be, I want to be water,
I'm trying to flow though I'm dense and silver,
I'm trying to move a ton of metal
as easily as the sea.

McGill Park, Summer

When the green shadows gasp, collapse to gold
     in the long arc of late afternoon,
The athletes are kicking a ball someone tossed
     from Sparta. I think I have always been here
In a moment of perpetual surrender,
     watching the dust clouds claim their heels
And waiting for some final sign to be revealed.
     Nearby, three silent statues submit
To spraying arcs of foam and I am lost
     among their perfect arms and heads.
Now with a small red bucket a child goes
     to catch some water from the wellspring
Of the gods.

A Dream

Below my naked foot I find
      a submerged statue's outstretched hand
In water only ankle deep where sullen gods
      float by beside a fallen house
Of which three pillars stand.

I don't know why you follow me
      to stumble over marble elbows,
      shallow hands.
Below me now the white gods die
      in this field of broken
Water where we stand.

The Real Name of the Sea

Everything would have been different
had I known it before. I would have had no fear
of tunnels, thunder, wind and water, also time,
which brought me always to the brink of being
and taught me how to love, and die.
(Sheer lightning found me cowering
hot and cold upon the floor; there were
some kinds of light I couldn't bear.
Even the candles lit for all the birthnights
of my life
were a blaze of boats in an ocean funeral)

I insisted that my terrifying cosmos
was not different from your own;
I promised you that it contained
all you had ever seen or done;
(for I had seen all things converge to one)
I asked you to hold the gold shell
of the burning sea to your ear
and hear the drowning children
call for their Viking fathers
and worldbreakers breaking
on the awful shores of love forever.

Everything would have been different
had I known it before. Thalassa —
(whisper with me) *Thalassa,*
these last of the world's children
beg pardon at your shores.

When You Come Upon Him

When you come upon him at the edge of the water,
child of Allah,
with wheels of light and all the bright leaves
of the world flying around him —
tell him that I served him well,
the handsome two-horned one who waits
at the river of the world's end.
Tell him I bore the seed which was his dream,
tell him I made havoc in his name.

Whenever the faceless winds were calling
the seed of the future from the world,
I with a mere breath would call
the liquid millions from his loins
to inhabit me briefly before they fell.

For the four winds made murder in my head
and the pebbles in the water were a million eyes.
I was possessed and cold. I cried: *O shed*
the secret generations from your loins
that these your ghostly children, Lord,
shall lead me by the hair
to the limits of the world.

Written After Coming Out of a Deep Sleep

How did I see the people of my dream when my eyes were closed?

You saw them with the eyes of your mind.

And now that I am awake do I see with my own eyes?

No. You are the eyes of my Mind, and you are here to help me see my Dream.

Apollo Twelve

Once his eye raised the cool towers of space
Over the roofs of his youth, and he lay
Growing in the red shifting days beneath
Orbiting castles and giants and starbeasts.

Now he descends the steep mountain of the night
To the breathless valley of the moon; earthlight
Floods the lunar pools and craters accommodate
The visitation of his step, his alien weight.

Earthrise is an eye beyond the blinding brim;
Past sighing miles of silence the finite children
Watch him become the satellite of his own dream
And orbit the white world of his youth for them.

Computers map the territories of nether suns
Where galaxies are graphic castles giants own;
Now up the weightless slopes of time he climbs
Through vacuous doorways to the gasping dark beyond.

THE
FIRE-EATERS

The Carnival

1

I danced before I learned to walk
And spoke before I learned to talk;
I can do almost anything
But me myself I cannot sing.
Who am I, and who
Lives in the carnival behind my eye?

I swallow swords, I swallow fire
Twice a day for a very small fee;
I am everyone's desire.
Do you know me?
I escape from ropes and chains
But I am not free, I am
The juggler juggling worlds behind your eye
I am the prisoner of me.

Who escapes from all the knots
The world can tie?
I swallow my words like swords
And cry
Who am I, and who
Lives in the carnival behind my eye?

2

I joined myself in the Mirror House
When all the children had gone home.
Hey! dancer, juggler, fire-eater, clown!
The crippled mirror stops you where you stand;
The mirror has just stolen your left hand
And the whole glass house comes tumbling down.

I dance alone, I asked to dance alone
Inside the silver mirrors of my mind
Inside the living prison of my bones.

3

The wheel of the carnival turns forever
And I am its crazy seasonal rider.
I can't get off it, either
For when I paid my fare I said:
I want a ticket for the endless ferris;
Let me on it, let me on!
And the man said; *It'll cost you plenty.*
And I answered:
I can't stand to see the great wheel empty,
Let me on it, let me on!
And he said: *Okay, man, it's your money.*

But it's funny because sometimes
I'm glad I can't get off it.
I circle, I rise, I fall.
I seem to move better than anyone below
Even though I can't move at all.

4

I danced before I learned to walk
And spoke before I learned to talk;
I can do almost anything
But me myself I cannot sing.
Who am I, and who
Lives in the carnival behind my eye?

The singer who falls back into the song
The dancer who falls back into the dance
Houdini who falls back into his chains
To imprison himself again,
To laugh.
Who lives in the carnival which is you?
I do, I do.

5

Ladies and gentlemen I'll dance for you
Twice a day for a very small fee
Or I'll break chains and swallow fire
If you follow me.
I'll juggle worlds before your eyes;
I am the way, I am the light.
Lock me up and I'll be free
To dance forever, if you follow me.

Animal Syllables

Let me say right off that this is no answer, for no question has as yet been posed. The gulls, merely, have gone mad out on the lake and have turned pure white for Christmas. Who has seen the future in retrospect? The lighthouse keeper at the end of the pier has nothing to say, and the great light rotates at the tip of the tower. The waves recur, the light, the seasons; memories flash and turn and guide the ships of wisdom in. I want to record the colours, the redness, the seagreen, the pure white; I want my syllables pure as the speech of gulls, or foxes.

The gulls are always screaming from the end of the long stone tongue which is the pier; the lake is always tasting the beach where once I lay beside the beachfire, my forehead facing Orion; the breakwater always chastises the waves, and the place where I pasted a poem with surf to a rock remains. It is earth, and surf, and blood; art is a small crime I commit against the seasons, or sometimes an elaborate lie my better sense rejoices in. And all the while the waves insist, present me with their patient, disciplined argument: *It has all been said before.* The rocks talk, and the lighthouse describes Cabbalistic arcs all over the darkness. What colour was I wearing in September when the beach turned infra-red a second before the sunset? A red sweater, I remember now, and I bent over a strange shell. I could see the veins of my hands beneath the flesh; a black steamer passed silently through the channel; the shameless sun streamed over my left shoulder and set. Everything seemed gentle, and wild; a single gull was the Holy Spirit, a savage dove; a white dog was the violent Lamb. Dark, I built a beachfire and thought about the flames and the earth. In the darkness I constructed a fire; in the midst of the fire I began to gather another darkness.

The two cats, Cagliostro and Sundog, are constantly repairing themselves, combing, pulling, licking; it's almost as if they are able to anticipate some sort of ultimate wound and heal it in advance. The waves take care of the rocks in the same way, although they wear away with so much attention. Do all the soothing tongues of mothers, and seas, and lovers melt and wear away the flesh and rock they seek to heal? Do we die thin from the thousand kisses that drive the hurt away?

Kazmatla, I whisper (it is a word I have made up), *Kazmatla. I believe. Life is red, it is many colours.* Beyond these words is a private dance. It is as silent as that.

I went one midnight to the geometric gardens. Lakelight, the moon on lake, brought out the depths of their colours, and I stood close to where some dark water trickled through concrete slots. I could see only the red midnight flowers and the black basins of the fountains behind them. The flowers smelled stronger from a distance than they did right under the nostrils. Cinnamon and honey, acid.

I bent down over the water slots and shouted something, and the syllables were liquid syllables; they flowed down and away, out of the garden, toward the lake. They became the lake. I felt myself proceeding with ease from one reality to another, imagined myself creating and destroying each world of sensation I encountered.

Some time later I boiled eggs and ate my thin volumes of verse like fragile lettuce sandwiches. Then I think I wrote again with raving sanity: 'The lake claims my face, the work of the surf is my body; I must remember those orderly, censured gardens...'

I have begun to repair the house, having put it off for ages, deciding which aspect of it was most in need of repair.

Of erections, how few are domed like St. Peter's? I ask myself (Melville), as I hammer nails into the tottering walls.

Are there too many realities? I ask, as several of the nails fall out.

Art is affirmation; to lift the pen is to say Yes! I cry, as the wall and I support each other.

Then I begin to bring the outside in, that the house might be a small, select museum of the world. In the summer I bring driftwood, shells, flowers. There is no key to this place and, in a sense, no door. There is free passage in and out. Already small weeds shoot up between the floor and the wall.

I tack up wallpaper that looks like wood (the walls were wood in the first place until the previous tenants covered them with dainty indoor scenes). I consider embroidering excerpts from the Cabbala on the cushion covers, or crocheting the writings of Kazantzakis on the tea-cosy, but I have no patience for such things. It seems I have one foot in one world and the other foot in another; I think I need new shoes.

Melville, it is said, read books about whales using whaleskins as bookmarks...

When the ice-sheets groan and split on the lake they fracture the landscape for miles around. Today I bless the authors of our borders and boundaries — Columbus who I sometimes imagine anchored in mid-sea with America moving out like a great ship to discover *him*. Vast shorelines, tongues of continents like land-waves chasing the seas. Shorelines of souls, the beaches of consciousness strewn with a thousand little shells. . .

The warehouses in the harbour turn gold at sunset; strange ships might sail in now from exotic foreign lands carrying ostrich feathers, elephant tusks, spices, silver filigreed bracelets, quinquireme. . . The snow-capped coalpiles are a mountain range in Tibet. Sundog the cat enters the house with snow on his eyebrows. All is well with the world. Somewhere out on the breakwater a single gull is preparing for some ultimate flight. Everything begins, everything is a continuum, everything organizes its death. There are red midnights of flowers, there are white midnights of snow. There are no alternatives to pain, there are no alternatives to beauty. The lighthouse describes great cryptic arcs across the darkness. We fold in upon ourselves like the waves, we fold under, falling in and out of the world's vision. How many languages can we know? We approach the end of utterance.

Kazmatla, Kazmatla, the waves insist it has all been said before. Somehow they must convince me, somehow I must believe them. The body has its own speech to be heeded now. Move swiftly in these snows, and leave no track.

THE
T. E. LAWRENCE
POEMS

The Absolute Room

We came to a place which was the center of ourselves
        in the desert between Aleppo and Hama;
We came to this Roman place where a hundred scents
        were built somehow right into the walls.
So the old man and the boy led us through courts
        of jasmine, and many other flowers, then
Into this great hall where all the scents slayed
        each other, and were still, and all
We breathed was pure desert air.

                    We call
      this room the sweetest of them all,
You said.
      And I thought: *Because there is nothing here.*

I knew then that you possessed nothing of me, and I
        possessed nothing of you, Dahoum.
We were wealthy and stuffed with a wondrous nothing
        that filled the room and everything around.

You looked into my eyes, the windows to my soul,
        and said that because they were blue
You could see right through them, holes in my skull,
        to the quiet, powerful sky beyond.

Thunder-Song

Two musicians played before the storm broke; one played
Wind-song, wind in the dry valley grass;
                                    one played
        dark, blind music on two strings. They both
Sang of war and love and death — what else is there
        to sing for?

Then came the armies of rain, wave after wave of it,
And a murderous blue lightning which brought the stones
        to life in the courtyard outside.
                                    Two lions
        on a pedestal laughed and laughed at us, with
        blue rain slobbering down their jaws, and then

Came the god, striding along an inscription towards the door.

The first musician controlled the thunder with his pipe
And the second explored the spaces in between
        the statements of the light.
                                In the place we were,
The place between twin rivers, Babylon, all was articulate
And utterly real.
                        Then the storm subsided and the pipe wept
At its passing. I knew that if ever I died it would be thus:

A helmetted seven-foot god coming quietly in blue light
Towards me.

The Virgin Warrior

When we rested between marches, I read Aristophanes
In the original Greek. I also had
                              Morte d'Arthur, and
The Oxford Book of English Verse.
                              Then came the day
        of the camel charge; we surged forward, swords
        raised like exclamation marks, and
        purple banners flying.
When the enemy became real, I got terribly excited
        and shot my camel through the head
        by accident, flew to the ground
And lay there with her as the army leapt over us,

Thinking, in lines as long as a camel's stride, of Kipling.

The Mirage

This is the desert, as I promised you.
　　There are no landmarks, only
Those you imagine, or those made by rocks
　　that fell from heaven.

Did you ever know where you were going?
　　Am I as invisible to you
As you always were to me, fellow traveller?
　　You are not here for nothing.

There are no easy ways of seeing, riding
　　the waves of invisible seas
In marvellous vessels which are always
　　arriving or departing.

I have come to uncover the famous secrets
　　of earth and water, air and fire.
I have come to explore and contain them all.
　　I am an eye.

I need tons of yellow space, and nothing
　　in the spectrum is unknown to me.
I am the living center of your sight; I draw for you
　　this thin and dangerous horizon.

Solar Wind

It comes upon you unawares —
                                    something racing out of the edge
Of your vision, as when you are staring at something
          and not staring — looking through —
A herd of white horses grazing on the periphery
Of your sight, and the afternoon
                             slanting into night —

Comes the wind that is
                       the colour of the sun, and your eyes
          which are nuggets of gold follow it
          down the barrels of the rifles, through
          the gun-cotton, and over the culverts,
Leaving everything gold, gold in its wake.

The past and the future are burning up; the present
          melts down the middle, a river of wind,
          wind from the sun, gold wind, anything —
And suddenly you know that all mysteries have been solved
          for you, all questions answered.

You must find a god to worship or you will die
In that unholy moment just before darkness and the sound
Of guns.

The Real Enemies

In that land where the soul aged long before the body,
My nameless men, my glamorous bodyguards,
                                        died for me.
My deadly friends with their rouged lips and pretty eyes
        died for me; *my bed of tulips* I called them,
        who wore every colour but the white
        that was mine alone to wear.

But they could not guard me against the real enemies —
Omnipotence, and the Infinite —
                        those beasts the soul invents
        and then bows down before.
The real enemies were not the men of Fakhri Pasha, nor
Were they even of this world.
                        One could never conquer them,
Never. Hope was another of them, Hope, most brutal of all.

For those who thought clearly, failure was the only goal.
Only failure could redeem you, there where the soul aged
        long before the body.
You failed at last, you fell into the delicious light
        and were free.

And there was much honour in this;
                        it was a worthy defeat.
Islam is surrender — the passionate surrender of the self,
        the puny self, to God.
We declared a Holy War upon Him and were victors as He won.

A Photograph From Carcemish

I gaze at you now, my darling, my brother,
     the pistol asleep in your young groin,
     your lips pulled back in a mighty grin.
My little Hittite, after you there can be no other.

In your dark eyes, my darling, my brother,
The world was created from the waters of Chaos;
     now black waves of tears
     crash upon the beaches of my sleep
     and drown my dreams forever.

Dahoum, Dahoum, Dahoum!

Damascus

The dream was dead in me before we reached Damascus;
      it died with your death, and dead love
Was all I carried around with me in the clumsy luggage
      of the desert. But I remember
Entering the city, and air silk with locusts;
      there was the smell of eternal cookies baking,
And someone ran up to me with a bunch of yellow grapes.

In the crowds, the Arabs smelled of dried sweat,
      and the English had a hot aura of piss
And naptha. For some reason I noticed a sword
      lying unused in a garden, a still garden
Behind a palm tree. And the worthless Turkish money
      was flying crazily through the air.
Later, in the evening, the satiny white sand cooled
      my feet; nowhere else was there such sand.

That night the Turks and Germans burned what was left
      of their ammunition dumps.
They're burning Damascus, I said. And then I fell asleep.

Clouds Hill

Over twenty miles of broken heath and a river valley
Full of rhododendrons, the Prince of Mecca comes home.
    At least I think I am at home, but
    even the house is travelling somewhere —
    through time, I think, and beyond.
What is exotic? Home is more exotic than anywhere.
Walking to Clouds Hill, I see the trees get crookeder
    and crookeder; their branches bridge
    the night and morning. Herds of clouds
Erase the sunset; I inhabit the hard core of everywhere.

The wind is easing south; soon, shy stars will come.
Everything has designed itself — the planets know me,
    wind knows me, night knows me;
    Clouds Hill leans against the sky.
I'm awaiting something so important it will never be,
And in dreams I go south and south and south again:
    Damascus, Deraa, Amman, Jerusalem,
    Beersheba, Ma'an, Akaba, Wejh, Um Lej,
    Yenbo, Rabegh, Jidda, Mecca.

Feisal is dead; Bob and Mother are still spreading God,
    and the news from China is nil.
Some of my diaries were written in pencil, upside-down,
    and day after day I decipher them
    on a heavy oak desk.
I live on dark chocolate, and write about the War.

Departures

Ghostly riders on blonde and dreaming camels
                                    drift
Out of the east side of my sight,
                              harbingers of morning.
I see again the sword in the still
                              garden
Behind the palm tree —
                    Feisal's sword, flashing. The air
Is silk with locusts;
                  then the drawn sword breaks the silk
And the sky heaves
                  open.

Night comes and the stars are out. Salaam.

Date